You are a person of consequence.

Be brave.

PRAISE FOR *THE BRAVE HABIT*:

"Todd's book will change the world we live in and the lives of the people who read it. Grab a copy for the people you care about, and save one for yourself."

SETH GODIN, author of *The Song of Significance*

"Every leader looking to make an impact needs this guide by their side. *The Brave Habit* is a roadmap for meaningful change."

DORIE CLARK, author of *The Long Game*

"I have read thousands of inspirational books over the years, but what set *The Brave Habit* apart is the way it drove me to make clear, concrete, and practical changes in my own life. If you want to be brave and make bolder moves right now, start with this book."

TOM RATH , author of *StrengthsFinder 2.0* and *Life's Great Question*

"Choosing to step forward when you want to step back ... that's the moment that saves the world and unlocks your greatness. This book helps you to be brave."

MICHAEL BUNGAY STANIER, author of *The Coaching Habit*

THE
BRAVE
HABIT
WORKBOOK
TODD HENRY

MARION HOUSE

Hello,

If you're choosing to do this workbook, it's because you want to engage more bravely with your life and work. By following the exercises within, you will gain clarity about what truly matters to you, the resources you have to be able to pursue those priorities, and which risks are worth taking in the process.

We need you to be *brave*.

Best,

Todd

ORIGINS

In the first section of *The Brave Habit*, I told the story of almost dying as a teenager. That experience certainly shaped my perspective on life and risk, and still influences many of my decisions today.

Sometimes, reflecting on past experiences can reveal character traits that we overlook in the hustle of daily life.

Think back on a time when you acted bravely, regardless of whether it felt brave at the time.

What happened?

_____

_____

_____

_____

_____

Why did you make the choice you made?

_____

_____

_____

_____

_____

What was the result?

_____

_____

_____

_____

_____

If given the chance, would you do it again? Why or why not?

_____

_____

_____

_____

_____

Take five minutes right now to consider your life and work.

Are there any areas where you suspect that you need to act bravely, but have been taking the easier path? Here are a few prompts to get you started:

Relationships

Projects

Career

Health

Family

Service

Neighborhood

THE COWARD

Inside of you lives a coward.

This coward is obsessed with self-preservation, self-protection, avoidance of risk, harm to reputation, failure, self-disappointment, and wishful thinking. The coward engages in frequent doubt, blame, regret, self-loathing, and catastrophizing.

But, also inside of you lives the capacity for unspeakable bravery.

Bravery is doing the right thing even in the face of fear, following intuition where it leads, acting where others shrink from opportunity, defending those who cannot defend themselves, boldly speaking your ideas into the world, and sacrificing what's necessary to bring them into existence.

No one aspires to cowardice, yet many still choose it every day. They fail to speak up because they're afraid of being wrong. They take the easier, more comfortable path instead of the one that could lead to immense return on their effort. They join the crowd instead of standing firm against the populist tide. They justify their cowardice as prudence.

Is there any place in your life or work where you are justifying your choices as "prudence" when they are actually based on comfort or avoiding doing the right thing?

What should you do as a result?

Remember: Bravery is not stupid risk. It's doing what's right, even when it's difficult.

BRAVERY IS ABOUT MOMENTS

Your moment is coming. It will be a time of testing for you of belief, character, will, strength, vision - and how you respond could prove an inflection point in your life, for better or worse.

However, your moment is probably not some major life change or big, public decision. Rather, it's likely to be a small, private test.

As you survey your upcoming week, what small, private tests of bravery do you anticipate might come up?

_____

_____

_____

_____

_____

Have you ever known someone who only did what was best for themselves? What happened to their relationships? Were they considered trust-worthy? Why or why not?

_____

_____

_____

_____

_____

BRAVERY IS A DISCIPLINE, NOT AN INEVITABLE OUTCOME.

Ironically, those with the most influence often become the most risk-averse. Every great organization began with someone taking a risk and creating something of value in spite of the odds. Then, once they have something to protect, many organizations huddle up, turn inward, and design their systems to protect what they've already done instead of seeking new frontiers to conquer.

In my experience, this often happens because the key leadership has become disconnected from the core values that drove the organization to achieve greatness in the first place. They have lost sight of their first love.

Is there any place in your life or work where you were once willing to take risks but have now become risk-averse? Why do you think that's the case?

_____

_____

_____

_____

_____

Do you believe that "bravery is a discipline rather than an inevitable outcome"? If not, why?

_____

_____

_____

_____

_____

What is something that used to require bravery, but that you now do with ease? What happened?

_____

_____

_____

_____

_____

_____

_____

_____

Bravery yields more bravery.

Have you ever been afraid to do something but changed your mind because you saw someone else do it? What was it, and what changed in you that caused you to act bravely?

_____

_____

_____

_____

_____

You convict others when you act on your convictions.

Similarly, others take their cues from you. Can you think of a time when you went *first* and others were encouraged to follow? What happened?

_____

_____

_____

_____

_____

_____

ACTION BREEDS CONFIDENCE & COURAGE –DALE CARNEGIE

THE HERO MYTH

> **Bravery is doing the right thing even in the face of fear or personal loss.**
>
> **Not in the absence of fear or potential for loss, but in the face of it. Acting bravely means understanding the cost of failure, but choosing to do the right thing regardless.**
>
> **Cowardice, on the other hand, is choosing self-protection over right action. Interestingly, it is possible to appear brave to others while actually behaving in a cowardly way. Someone can posture their decision as brave, but secretly be operating selfishly. This isn't bravery, it's just boldness.**

In your own words, describe the difference between bravery and boldness. How are their effects different?

_____

_____

_____

_____

_____

Have you ever done something that others thought was brave, but you secretly knew it wasn't? What happened?

_____

_____

_____

_____

_____

Inversely, have you ever been accused of being a coward when you were actually being brave? What happened?

_____

_____

_____

_____

_____

_____

Bravery is always empathetic.

If your actions are purely selfish, they may be bold but not necessarily brave. Think about someone in your life right now who could use brave action on their behalf. Who is it, and what could you do to help them?

_____

_____

_____

_____

_____

A key requirement for brave action is uncertainty. If outcomes were guaranteed, there would be no need for bravery.

As you consider your life and work, where do you feel the most uncertainty at the moment? Why?

_____

_____

_____

_____

_____

Bravery exists when we have a vision for a better possible future, and we trust that we have agency to help bring it about.

In those areas of uncertainty listed above, what does your vision of a "better possible future" look like? And, are there actions you can take within your sphere of influence to help bring about those outcomes?

_____

_____

_____

_____

_____

_____

_____

As you consider the "Cowardice Quadrants", which one resonates the most with you right now? Why?

_____

_____

_____

_____

_____

_____

_____

_____

_____

_____

_____

_____

_____

_____

_____

_____

HIGH PERCEIVED AGENCY

NIHILISM / FUTILITY   **BRAVERY!**

PESSIMISM   OPTIMISTIC VISION

RESIGNATION   VICTIMHOOD

LOW PERCEIVED AGENCY

The **BRAVE** habit is comprised of five key parts:

1. **Block** time for reflection.

2. **Review** your life and work.

3. Take **agency**.

4. **Visualize** your better possible future.

5. **Express** your intent and mission for the week.

Right now, take ten minutes to engage in your first Brave Habit review.

1. Block time for reflection. (That's now, so we'll skip this step. However, you are encouraged to plan fifteen minutes per week for this exercise.)

2. Review your life and work.

Below are a few prompts. Over time, you'll develop your own.

What uncertainties are you facing right now? What's giving you anxiety?

Where are the next steps unclear?

Where is there relational tension, or a lack of resolution?

Which projects on the horizon intimidate you?

Which conversations do you know you need to have, but are avoiding?

_____

_____

_____

_____

_____

3. Take agency.

As you consider each of your answers above:

What capacity do you have to influence the outcome?

_____

_____

_____

_____

_____

What is an acceptable risk in each situation, and what's unacceptable?

_____

_____

_____

_____

_____

_____

What new skill or aptitude might help you better address the uncertainty?

_____

_____

_____

_____

_____

_____

_____

_____

4. Visualize your better possible future.

As you consider your life and work, and the uncertainties above:

What would a "better possible future" look like for each?

_____
_____
_____
_____
_____
_____
_____

What values do you live by, and how do they apply to each of the situations above?

_____
_____
_____
_____
_____
_____
_____

Where have you been compromising your values due to pressure, comfort, or carelessness?

_____
_____
_____
_____
_____
_____
_____
_____
_____
_____
_____

5. Express your intent and mission.

For each area listed above:

What brave action can you take in each area?

_____

_____

_____

_____

_____

_____

_____

_____

_____

_____

Who will hold you accountable for acting?

_____

_____

_____

_____

IN THE MOMENT OF UNCERTAINTY, WHAT YOU *TRULY* BELIEVE IS REVEALED.

CULTIVATING AGENCY

Consider the things you feel anxious about. Which of them are in your "Circle of Concern", but outside of your "Circle of Influence"?

Is there any place in your life or work where you feel powerless over the situation? What is it, and why do you feel that way?

Where do you feel the most insecure or "out of your league" in your daily life or work? Is there a skill or some kind of knowledge that would help you feel more capable?

Consider one skill that you're going to develop over the next three months. Then, choose a method for learning it, and plot a plan of action. Measure your progress so that you know how you're doing along the way.

The skill:

_____

_____

The method:

_____

_____

How will you measure progress?

_____

_____

_____

_____

Do the people you spend time with encourage you to grow, or reinforce bad habits? Who most encourages growth, and how do they do it?

_____

_____

_____

_____

_____

_____

Who do you call upon for wisdom in a moment of uncertainty? When was the last time, and what was the result?

_____

_____

_____

Who was the last person you truly encouraged? What happened?

_____
_____
_____
_____
_____
_____
_____
_____
_____

Where have you earned trust that gives you the right to speak your ideas? How have you leveraged it?

_____
_____
_____
_____
_____
_____
_____
_____

What audience has given you permission to share ideas with them?

_____
_____
_____
_____
_____
_____

Who are the people that are "rooting" for you? How do they support you?

_____
_____
_____
_____
_____
_____

What unique resources do you have that others don't that you can leverage toward your goals?

_____

_____

_____

_____

_____

▌ ***As your platform grows, so does the perceived cost of action.***

Is there any place where you're afraid to act because of the perceived cost of getting it wrong?

_____

_____

_____

_____

_____

_____

_____

_____

In what areas do you seem to have outsized influence compared to your peers? Or, where do you have more credibility than others?

_____

_____

_____

_____

_____

_____

_____

_____

What small, brave action could you take today to help you move toward your goals?

_____

_____

_____

_____

_____

THE BRAVE HABIT WORKBOOK

Have you ever made a good decision that had a bad outcome? What happened? What did you learn?

_____

_____

_____

_____

_____

_____

_____

_____

While most adults have mastered physical brachiation, psychological brachiation can be much more difficult to embrace. Much like the fearful child on the monkey bars, when we lack the ability to let go of the way things have been and move on to something new, we get stuck. We stall our momentum. While we may not be in physical harm, we spend months or years spinning our wheels, hopelessly stuck in place, unable to move forward. In our desire to maintain stability by remaining rooted in the present/past, we undermine our future potential.

Is there anything in your life (a loss, a disappointment, a failure) that you have a hard time letting go of and moving past? What happened, and how does it affect you?

_____

_____

_____

_____

_____

_____

_____

_____

What does bravely "letting go" look like?

_____

_____

_____

_____

There's a more subtle form of brave action that in some ways looks like inaction - bravery to wait. Sometimes the most brave decision you can make is to stand firm against the tide, even

when everything around you is trending in the other direction. You may feel like you're missing out on a golden opportunity, or others may tell you that you are foolish to pause, but you know deep down that it's not the right time. Your particular act of bravery is to stand against popular opinion or critique.

Is there any situation where you feel the need to rush in, but are actually only doing so because it's the popular thing to do? What does bravery look like in that situation?

_____

_____

_____

_____

_____

_____

_____

_____

_____

_____

Patience is often its own form of bravery.

What brave action have you been deferring because you don't believe you have the agency to act? Is it true patience, or are you rationalizing?

_____

_____

_____

_____

_____

_____

_____

_____

_____

_____

The most predictable driver of optimism is productive passion. This is an outcome that you care so deeply about that you are willing to suffer if necessary to achieve it. It is clean fuel.

The Brave Habit offers a few questions to help you identify your "productive passion", or the outcome that you're willing to pursue even if it costs you.

What is a primal belief that you hold, even if others think it's crazy?

_____

_____

_____

_____

_____

What moves you emotionally, even if others don't seem to notice?

_____

_____

_____

_____

What are you unwilling to compromise on, no matter the cost?

_____

_____

_____

_____

PRODUCTIVE PASSION IS CLEAN FUEL.

A brave question is one that you don't necessarily want the answer to.

Below is a list of brave questions. Choose three, and answer them on the next page:

Is this true, or do I just want it to be true?

If it's not true, is it possible to make it true?

How do I need to improve as a leader/creator/employee/

human being?

What do I suspect but am afraid to admit?

What if it was my fault?

What if it wasn't my fault?

What would I do if I wasn't afraid?

What am I willing to sacrifice in order to see it happen?

How can I make it right?

What if that's a false assumption?

Should I step up and lead?

Should I step down and let someone else take charge?

Is this confidence, or ego speaking?

Who could I ask for help?

What kind of person/leader/team member do I want to be?

BRAVE QUESTIONS

Where in your life or work are you stalled because you lack a clear vision in the face of uncertainty? How could you clarify that vision?

_____

_____

_____

_____

_____

_____

_____

_____

_____

_____

_____

Action Step: Think about an important decision you are facing. How can you filter that decision through your productive passion in order to gain clarity? What is your vision of a better possible future?

_____

_____

_____

_____

_____

_____

_____

_____

_____

_____

_____

_____

_____

_____

_____

_____

BRAVE WORK

You are not your work, in that it is not the sum of your identity. But in many ways, you are your work, because it's an expression of what you believe. Your body of work stands as a lasting testament to where you chose to spend your finite time, attention, and energy, and the impact that it has will long outlast your physical time on this planet. It will echo for years to come in the lives of the people you influence.

Are you building a body of work you can point to with pride? Is it representative of your values and aspirations, or is it the sum of your greatest compromises?

Imagine yourself many years in the future, looking back on your life and work. What words would you use to describe the difference that you made on the planet? (Think beyond just your job. Consider your relationships, family, service, etc.)

_____

_____

_____

_____

_____

_____

_____

_____

Have you ever encountered someone who refused to own their words and actions? How did that affect your relationship?

_____

_____

_____

_____

_____

_____

_____

Is there any place where you are struggling to own your words and actions? What can you do about it?

_____

_____

_____

_____

_____

_____

_____

_____

_____

> **To encourage literally means to "put courage into" others. Brave people embolden the people around them, speak words of affirmation to them, and cheer them on to be their best. They are not threatened by the successes of others.**

Who puts courage into you? Have you thanked them? (How could you?)

_____

_____

_____

_____

Who could you encourage this week? How will you do it?

_____

_____

_____

_____

_____

_____

Some people fear trying new things, learning new skills, or tackling new kinds of projects because they fear that if they fail they will be "found out". Brave people know that occasional failure is simply a part of doing hard things.

When was the last time you failed while trying something difficult? What was it, and what happened?

_____

_____

_____

_____

_____

_____

_____

_____

Have you been avoiding anything difficult out of a fear of failing?

_____

_____

_____

You cannot control whether someone else likes your ideas, but you can control whether or not you share them. The regret for inaction is too high a price to pay.

In my work with high capacity teams, one common thread among those who are especially effective is that they are quick to share ideas with one another, even before those ideas are fully formed.

Is there an idea that you've been afraid to share because you don't know how it will be received? What would truly happen if you shared it? Who should you share it with?

_____

_____

_____

_____

Brave people do what's right, even when it might cost them everything they've worked for.

If you are willing to compromise your values in small ways in order to avoid discomfort, you set yourself up to compromise in much larger, more damaging ways later. Be a person who acts upon their convictions, even when it might cost you.

When you are under pressure, and facing uncertainty, you are most vulnerable to compromising your deepest held values. So, it's worth considering those values prior to experiencing those moments.

_____

_____

_____

_____

_____

_____

What are the values that you bring to your life, your work, and your decisions that frame up your decision-making?

_____

_____

_____

_____

_____

_____

_____

_____

_____

_____

_____

_____

_____

_____

_____

_____

_____

As you consider your work and your career, are you approaching it with a finite, or an infinite mindset? Are you simply competing against others in order to get the next promotion, or is there something else you are pursuing that transcends the temporary wins and losses you experience along the way? Cowards climb the ladder because of what it brings them in terms of comfort and accolades. Brave people are driven by principles and cause.

The Brave Habit discussed James Carse's concept of "finite" and "infinite" games. What infinite game are you playing through your work? What greater cause or good are you pursuing?

BRAVE TEAMS

Brave action tends to lead to more brave action. When you act bravely, you give me permission to do the same.

Who challenges you to be brave? Have you thanked them?

_____

_____

_____

_____

_____

_____

Do you have any open disagreements with colleagues that need to be resolved? What happened, and how will you approach the conversation?

_____

_____

_____

_____

_____

_____

Is there any place where you are avoiding conflict or trying to pre-maturely squash it in order to avoid discomfort?

_____

_____

_____

_____

_____

_____

_____

Has someone ever blamed you for something in order to protect their own reputation? How did it feel? How might you have acted differently in their situation?

What investments could you make in other people today? How might you encourage and elevate others in order to cultivate an environment in which brave action is more likely?

> **Brave teammates are willing to hear feedback they disagree with and are not afraid to offer helpful feedback when they believe a fellow teammate is not living up to their potential. No one wins when we hide the truth in order to be liked. This is putting yourself ahead of the productive passion of the team. Instead, be willing to risk being unliked for a season if it means helping others become better and achieve their desired results.**

Is there any feedback that you need to give someone else, but have been avoiding? When will you have the conversation?

BRAVE LEADERS

As a leader, you may think that your job is to get the work done. It's not.

Your job is to create an environment in which others can get the work done. Your job isn't to do the work, it's to lead the work. These are fundamentally different responsibilities.

And, a primary function of that responsibility is cultivating an environment that is conducive to brave action. This means that you consistently (a) fuel and refine a vision of a better possible future, and (b) speak agency into those who are responsible for helping bring it about.

As you consider those you lead, what can you do to speak agency and optimistic vision into them this week? Consider each person, and an action step you can take.

_____

_____

_____

_____

_____

_____

_____

Is there a difficult conversation that you need to initiate? What is it, and when will you take action? How might it be affecting your team's clarity about what you value, or their willingness to trust you?

_____

_____

_____

_____

_____

_____

_____

_____

_____

What is something you know you need to talk about with your own manager, but have been avoiding because it will be uncomfortable or could result in conflict?

_____

_____

_____

_____

_____

_____

_____

Is there any work that your team is doing that is under-resourced? How can you approach your team to discover areas where they have unmet needs?

_____

_____

_____

_____

_____

_____

Are you protecting your role, or giving it away? How can you develop other leaders on your team or in your organization?

_____

_____

_____

_____

_____

_____

_____

_____

_____

_____

BRAVE NEIGHBORS

If change is going to happen for the better, it will begin in our neighborhoods. We can commit to engaging bravely with one another, protecting one another, and forming alliances that help us stand for common values. We can re-humanize, re-connect, and engage in brave conversations with others who may (gasp!) disagree with our perspective. Doing so doesn't mean we have to end in agreement, but only that we are able to find common ground in the larger principles that bind us together.

Do you seek out relationships with people in your sphere of influence who don't necessarily think or look like you? If so, how has that shaped your perspective? If not, how can you begin?

_____

_____

_____

_____

_____

_____

_____

What would it look like for you to become a protector in your neighborhood?

_____

_____

_____

_____

_____

_____

_____

_____

_____

_____

_____

What "unseen" actions might you commit to as an act of service to your neighborhood?

_____
_____
_____
_____
_____
_____
_____
_____
_____
_____
_____
_____
_____
_____

What one brave action can you take this week to be a better neighbor?

_____
_____
_____
_____
_____
_____
_____
_____
_____
_____
_____
_____
_____
_____
_____
_____
_____
_____

BRAVE NEW WORLD

We each stand at various precipices in our lives, and in those moments we must choose our identity. Will you be the kind of person who shrinks from the moment, or the one who is willing - even when it's uncomfortable - to do the right thing? Will you not only endure, but embrace discomfort for the sake of the greater good? Will you refuse to rationalize cowardly behavior as an expression of wisdom?

Will you respond to the name "brave"?

What "precipice" are you standing at right now that might require brave action?

_____

_____

If you knew you had exactly one year left on this planet, what would you do? And, why aren't you doing it? To be fair, we have to behave responsibly and with an eye on the future, which is why I despise the advice "live each day like it's your last." However, as you consider your ideas, your dreams, your relationships, your ambitions, which of them are you deferring action on until a more convenient time? In truth, that time may never come.

1. On the following page, write the date at the top of the page.

2. Spend about ten minutes considering what you'd like to be different on that date. How will you have changed? Who will you have impacted? What will you have built?

3. Now, cross out anything that is outside of your sphere of influence. Don't focus on what you can't control.

4. With the remaining items, write one small action step that you can take in the next week to begin you on the journey of accomplishing it. The key is to make it small. It should almost feel easy.

5. Once you take your small step, write another one down. Then, do it.

Don't fear wrong action, fear inaction. Stagnancy is the specter that should keep you awake at night more than any other.

One small step in the face of fear is enough to dispel its hold on you. Regular, measured steps in the direction of your optimistic vision is sufficient to generate unstoppable momentum. When your big breakthrough comes, it probably won't feel momentous. Rather, it will seem like the next logical step in a long chain of brave actions. Success comes in layers and is earned through consistency. Consistency breeds confidence, which breeds courage. And consistency begins with a choice to show up and seize the moment.

So, what will you do with your one day? What small, brave actions will you choose?

Will you choose to be a reconciler of relationships by forgiving instead of assigning blame?

Will you choose to share your idea with your manager instead of giving in to the fear of ridicule?

Will you choose to make something - anything - that moves you closer to your long-deferred ambition instead of saying "someday I'll..."?

Will you choose to approach that client who seems out of reach instead of falling prey to imposter syndrome?

Each of these choices, and thousands of others in your life, are singular moments in time that establish a new vector for you. What you choose to do with them will ultimately determine whether you build a body of work you can point to with pride, or one which reflects your complacency, fear, and lack of nerve.

I cannot emphasize enough how urgent this day is for you.

You must treat it like your only valuable asset, because it is.

And within that precious day is a singular moment for you to seize.

What is it, and what will you do with it?

Be brave.

On the following pages, you will find additional space to engage in the Brave Habit.

Spend time each week considering how you will approach moments of uncertainty so that you are prepared to act bravely and with purpose.

WEEK OF: _____

REVIEW

What uncertainties are you facing right now? What's giving you anxiety?

_____

_____

_____

Where are the next steps unclear?

_____

_____

_____

_____

Where is there relational tension, or a lack of resolution?

_____

_____

_____

Which projects on the horizon intimidate you?

_____

_____

_____

Which conversations do you know you need to have, but are avoiding?

_____

_____

_____

_____

_____

_____

_____

_____

TAKE AGENCY

As you consider each of your answers above:

What capacity do you have to influence the outcome?

What is an acceptable risk in each situation, and what's unacceptable?

What new skill or aptitude might help you better address the uncertainty?

VISUALIZE A BETTER POSSIBLE FUTURE

As you consider your life and work, and the uncertainties above:

What would a "better possible future" look like for each?

_____

_____

_____

_____

_____

_____

_____

What values do you live by, and how do they apply to each of the situations above?

_____

_____

_____

_____

_____

_____

_____

Where have you been compromising your values due to pressure, comfort, or carelessness?

_____

_____

_____

_____

_____

_____

_____

_____

_____

_____

EXPRESS YOUR INTENT AND MISSION

For each area listed above:

What brave action can you take in each area?

Who will hold you accountable for acting?

WEEK OF: _____

REVIEW

What uncertainties are you facing right now? What's giving you anxiety?

_____

_____

_____

Where are the next steps unclear?

_____

_____

_____

_____

Where is there relational tension, or a lack of resolution?

_____

_____

_____

Which projects on the horizon intimidate you?

_____

_____

_____

Which conversations do you know you need to have, but are avoiding?

_____

_____

_____

_____

_____

_____

_____

_____

_____

TAKE AGENCY

As you consider each of your answers above:

What capacity do you have to influence the outcome?

_____

_____

_____

_____

_____

What is an acceptable risk in each situation, and what's unacceptable?

_____

_____

_____

_____

_____

_____

_____

_____

_____

_____

_____

_____

_____

_____

What new skill or aptitude might help you better address the uncertainty?

_____

_____

_____

_____

VISUALIZE A BETTER POSSIBLE FUTURE

As you consider your life and work, and the uncertainties above:

What would a "better possible future" look like for each?

What values do you live by, and how do they apply to each of the situations above?

Where have you been compromising your values due to pressure, comfort, or carelessness?

THE BRAVE HABIT WORKBOOK

EXPRESS YOUR INTENT AND MISSION

For each area listed above:

What brave action can you take in each area?

_____

_____

_____

_____

_____

_____

_____

_____

_____

_____

_____

_____

Who will hold you accountable for acting?

_____

_____

_____

_____

_____

_____

_____

_____

_____

_____

_____

_____

WEEK OF: _____

REVIEW

What uncertainties are you facing right now? What's giving you anxiety?

_____

_____

_____

Where are the next steps unclear?

_____

_____

_____

_____

Where is there relational tension, or a lack of resolution?

_____

_____

_____

Which projects on the horizon intimidate you?

_____

_____

_____

Which conversations do you know you need to have, but are avoiding?

_____

_____

_____

_____

_____

_____

_____

_____

TAKE AGENCY

As you consider each of your answers above:

What capacity do you have to influence the outcome?

What is an acceptable risk in each situation, and what's unacceptable?

What new skill or aptitude might help you better address the uncertainty?

VISUALIZE A BETTER POSSIBLE FUTURE

As you consider your life and work, and the uncertainties above:

What would a "better possible future" look like for each?

What values do you live by, and how do they apply to each of the situations above?

Where have you been compromising your values due to pressure, comfort, or carelessness?

EXPRESS YOUR INTENT AND MISSION

For each area listed above:

What brave action can you take in each area?

_____

_____

_____

_____

_____

_____

_____

_____

_____

_____

_____

_____

_____

Who will hold you accountable for acting?

_____

_____

_____

_____

_____

_____

_____

_____

_____

_____

_____

_____

_____

WEEK OF: _____

REVIEW

What uncertainties are you facing right now? What's giving you anxiety?

_____
_____
_____

Where are the next steps unclear?

_____
_____
_____
_____

Where is there relational tension, or a lack of resolution?

_____
_____
_____

Which projects on the horizon intimidate you?

_____
_____
_____

Which conversations do you know you need to have, but are avoiding?

_____
_____
_____
_____
_____
_____
_____
_____

TAKE AGENCY

As you consider each of your answers above:

What capacity do you have to influence the outcome?

What is an acceptable risk in each situation, and what's unacceptable?

What new skill or aptitude might help you better address the uncertainty?

VISUALIZE A BETTER POSSIBLE FUTURE

As you consider your life and work, and the uncertainties above:

What would a "better possible future" look like for each?

_____

_____

_____

_____

_____

_____

_____

What values do you live by, and how do they apply to each of the situations above?

_____

_____

_____

_____

_____

_____

_____

Where have you been compromising your values due to pressure, comfort, or carelessness?

_____

_____

_____

_____

_____

_____

_____

_____

_____

THE BRAVE HABIT WORKBOOK

EXPRESS YOUR INTENT AND MISSION

For each area listed above:

What brave action can you take in each area?

_____
_____
_____
_____
_____
_____
_____
_____
_____
_____
_____
_____
_____

Who will hold you accountable for acting?

_____
_____
_____
_____
_____
_____
_____
_____
_____
_____
_____
_____
_____

WEEK OF: _____

REVIEW

What uncertainties are you facing right now? What's giving you anxiety?

_____

_____

_____

Where are the next steps unclear?

_____

_____

_____

_____

Where is there relational tension, or a lack of resolution?

_____

_____

_____

Which projects on the horizon intimidate you?

_____

_____

Which conversations do you know you need to have, but are avoiding?

_____

_____

_____

_____

_____

_____

_____

_____

_____

THE BRAVE HABIT WORKBOOK

TAKE AGENCY

As you consider each of your answers above:

What capacity do you have to influence the outcome?

_____

_____

_____

_____

_____

What is an acceptable risk in each situation, and what's unacceptable?

_____

_____

_____

_____

_____

_____

_____

_____

_____

_____

_____

_____

_____

_____

What new skill or aptitude might help you better address the uncertainty?

_____

_____

_____

_____

VISUALIZE A BETTER POSSIBLE FUTURE

As you consider your life and work, and the uncertainties above:

What would a "better possible future" look like for each?

_____

_____

_____

_____

_____

_____

_____

What values do you live by, and how do they apply to each of the situations above?

_____

_____

_____

_____

_____

_____

_____

Where have you been compromising your values due to pressure, comfort, or carelessness?

_____

_____

_____

_____

_____

_____

_____

_____

_____

_____

EXPRESS YOUR INTENT AND MISSION

For each area listed above:

What brave action can you take in each area?

_____

_____

_____

_____

_____

_____

_____

_____

_____

_____

_____

_____

Who will hold you accountable for acting?

_____

_____

_____

_____

_____

_____

_____

_____

_____

_____

_____

_____

_____

WEEK OF: _____

REVIEW

What uncertainties are you facing right now? What's giving you anxiety?

_____

_____

_____

Where are the next steps unclear?

_____

_____

_____

_____

Where is there relational tension, or a lack of resolution?

_____

_____

_____

Which projects on the horizon intimidate you?

_____

_____

_____

Which conversations do you know you need to have, but are avoiding?

_____

_____

_____

_____

_____

_____

_____

_____

TAKE AGENCY

As you consider each of your answers above:

What capacity do you have to influence the outcome?

_____

_____

_____

_____

What is an acceptable risk in each situation, and what's unacceptable?

_____

_____

_____

_____

_____

_____

_____

_____

_____

_____

_____

_____

_____

What new skill or aptitude might help you better address the uncertainty?

_____

_____

_____

_____

VISUALIZE A BETTER POSSIBLE FUTURE

As you consider your life and work, and the uncertainties above:

What would a "better possible future" look like for each?

What values do you live by, and how do they apply to each of the situations above?

Where have you been compromising your values due to pressure, comfort, or carelessness?

EXPRESS YOUR INTENT AND MISSION

For each area listed above:

What brave action can you take in each area?

_____
_____
_____
_____
_____
_____
_____
_____
_____
_____
_____
_____
_____
_____

Who will hold you accountable for acting?

_____
_____
_____
_____
_____
_____
_____
_____
_____
_____
_____
_____
_____
_____

WEEK OF: _____

REVIEW

What uncertainties are you facing right now? What's giving you anxiety?

_____

_____

Where are the next steps unclear?

_____

_____

_____

Where is there relational tension, or a lack of resolution?

_____

_____

Which projects on the horizon intimidate you?

_____

_____

Which conversations do you know you need to have, but are avoiding?

_____

_____

_____

_____

_____

_____

_____

TAKE AGENCY

As you consider each of your answers above:

What capacity do you have to influence the outcome?

_____

_____

_____

_____

_____

What is an acceptable risk in each situation, and what's unacceptable?

_____

_____

_____

_____

_____

_____

_____

_____

_____

_____

_____

_____

_____

_____

_____

_____

What new skill or aptitude might help you better address the uncertainty?

_____

_____

_____

_____

VISUALIZE A BETTER POSSIBLE FUTURE

As you consider your life and work, and the uncertainties above:

What would a "better possible future" look like for each?

_____

_____

_____

_____

_____

_____

_____

What values do you live by, and how do they apply to each of the situations above?

_____

_____

_____

_____

_____

_____

_____

Where have you been compromising your values due to pressure, comfort, or carelessness?

_____

_____

_____

_____

_____

_____

_____

_____

_____

_____

EXPRESS YOUR INTENT AND MISSION

For each area listed above:

What brave action can you take in each area?

_____

_____

_____

_____

_____

_____

_____

_____

_____

_____

_____

_____

_____

_____

Who will hold you accountable for acting?

_____

_____

_____

_____

_____

_____

_____

_____

_____

_____

_____

_____

_____

WEEK OF: _____

REVIEW

What uncertainties are you facing right now? What's giving you anxiety?

_____

_____

_____

Where are the next steps unclear?

_____

_____

_____

_____

Where is there relational tension, or a lack of resolution?

_____

_____

_____

Which projects on the horizon intimidate you?

_____

_____

_____

Which conversations do you know you need to have, but are avoiding?

_____

_____

_____

_____

_____

_____

_____

_____

TAKE AGENCY

As you consider each of your answers above:

What capacity do you have to influence the outcome?

What is an acceptable risk in each situation, and what's unacceptable?

What new skill or aptitude might help you better address the uncertainty?

VISUALIZE A BETTER POSSIBLE FUTURE

As you consider your life and work, and the uncertainties above:

What would a "better possible future" look like for each?

_____

_____

_____

_____

_____

_____

What values do you live by, and how do they apply to each of the situations above?

_____

_____

_____

_____

_____

_____

Where have you been compromising your values due to pressure, comfort, or carelessness?

_____

_____

_____

_____

_____

_____

_____

_____

EXPRESS YOUR INTENT AND MISSION

For each area listed above:

What brave action can you take in each area?

_____

_____

_____

_____

_____

_____

_____

_____

_____

_____

_____

_____

Who will hold you accountable for acting?

_____

_____

_____

_____

_____

_____

_____

_____

_____

_____

_____

_____

WEEK OF: _____

REVIEW

What uncertainties are you facing right now? What's giving you anxiety?

_____

_____

_____

Where are the next steps unclear?

_____

_____

_____

_____

Where is there relational tension, or a lack of resolution?

_____

_____

_____

Which projects on the horizon intimidate you?

_____

_____

_____

Which conversations do you know you need to have, but are avoiding?

_____

_____

_____

_____

_____

_____

_____

_____

_____

TAKE AGENCY

As you consider each of your answers above:

What capacity do you have to influence the outcome?

_____

_____

_____

_____

What is an acceptable risk in each situation, and what's unacceptable?

_____

_____

_____

_____

_____

_____

_____

_____

_____

_____

_____

_____

_____

_____

What new skill or aptitude might help you better address the uncertainty?

_____

_____

_____

_____

VISUALIZE A BETTER POSSIBLE FUTURE

As you consider your life and work, and the uncertainties above:

What would a "better possible future" look like for each?

What values do you live by, and how do they apply to each of the situations above?

Where have you been compromising your values due to pressure, comfort, or carelessness?

EXPRESS YOUR INTENT AND MISSION

For each area listed above:

What brave action can you take in each area?

_____

_____

_____

_____

_____

_____

_____

_____

_____

_____

_____

_____

Who will hold you accountable for acting?

_____

_____

_____

_____

_____

_____

_____

_____

_____

_____

_____

THE BRAVE HABIT WORKBOOK

THE BRAVE HABIT WORKBOOK

THE BRAVE HABIT WORKBOOK

THE BRAVE HABIT WORKBOOK

THE BRAVE HABIT WORKBOOK

THE BRAVE HABIT WORKBOOK

THE BRAVE HABIT WORKBOOK

THE BRAVE HABIT WORKBOOK

THE BRAVE HABIT WORKBOOK